STAR WARS.

STAR WARS®

STAR WARS®

STARWARS®

STARWARS®

STAR WARS®

STAR WARS.

STAR WARS.

STARWARS®

STAR WARS.

STARWARS®

STARWARS

STARWARS®

STARWARS.

STARWARS®

STARWARS®

STAR WARS.

STARWARS.

STAR WARS®

STARWARS.

STAR WARS®

STARWARS.

STARWARS®

STAR WARS.®

STAR WARS.

STAR WARS®

STARWARS.

STARWARS®

STAR WARS ®

STARWARS®